SEVEN LAWS OF PURPOSE ATTAINMENT

Discovering Your Life's True Meaning And Fulfillment

OSCAR SYLVAN

or fitness for a particular purpose. No warranty may be created or extended by sales representatives or written sales materials. The advice and strategies contained herein may not be suitable for your situation. You should consult with a professional when appropriate. Neither the publisher nor the author shall be liable for any loss of profit or any other commercial damages, including but not limited to special, incidental, consequential, personal, or other damages.

Table of Contents

Introduction

Table of Contents

Introduction

Welcome to a Life of Purpose

In the vast tapestry of existence, each one of us is born with a unique thread—a thread that weaves its way through the intricate design of our lives, adding color, texture, and meaning to the world. This thread is our purpose, our reason for being, and it is waiting patiently for us to unravel its full potential.

Welcome to a journey of self-discovery and transformation—a journey that will lead you to the heart of your existence and set you on a course towards a life of profound purpose. Within the pages of this book, we will explore the Seven Laws of Purpose Attainment, a roadmap that will guide you toward a deeper understanding of yourself and your place in the world.

In the hustle and bustle of our daily lives, it's all too easy to lose sight of our purpose, to become entangled in the web of obligations, expectations, and distractions that surround us. We may find ourselves drifting aimlessly, yearning for something more, something that gives our lives true meaning and fulfillment. If you have ever experienced this, you are not alone.

But fear not, for the answers you seek are within your reach. Through the Seven Laws of Purpose Attainment, we will delve into the profound wisdom of purpose-driven living. We will learn how to clarify our deepest desires, align our actions with our values, and set meaningful goals that lead us toward our purpose. We will explore the power of self-awareness, resilience, and the importance of nurturing meaningful relationships. We will discover the joy that comes from taking purposeful action and the fulfillment that arises from living a life of purpose.

Throughout this journey, you will find practical exercises, real-life stories, and timeless principles that will empower you to embark on your quest for purpose. Whether you are at the beginning of your journey or seeking to deepen your sense of purpose, this book is a companion that will illuminate your path.

Are you ready to explore on this transformative journey? Are you ready to unlock the potential within you and embrace a life of purpose? If so, turn the page, and let's begin. Welcome to a life of purpose—a life where your unique thread can shine brightly in the grand tapestry of existence.

Chapter 1

The Power of Clarity

In the grand pursuit of purpose, clarity is the compass that guides us through the uncharted territories of our inner selves. It is the first step on the path towards living a life driven by intention and meaning. Within this chapter, we will delve deep into the fundamental aspects of clarity, exploring its transformative influence on our journey toward purpose attainment.

Understanding Your Why

Before we can navigate the path of purpose, we must first understand the fundamental question: Why are we

here? This question has intrigued philosophers, thinkers, and seekers of truth for millennia. It is a question that transcends the boundaries of time and culture, resonating with each of us on a deeply personal level.

Understanding your "why" goes beyond mere introspection; it requires a willingness to explore the depths of your beliefs, values, and aspirations. It involves peeling away the layers of societal expectations and external pressures to uncover your authentic self. Your "why" is the core motivation that fuels your actions, decisions, and ultimately, your purpose. It is the North Star that guides you when you find yourself adrift in the sea of uncertainty.

Throughout this chapter, we will embark on a journey of self-discovery to unearth your personal "why." We will explore the experiences, passions, and values that have shaped your life and continue to shape your desires. By understanding your "why," you will gain the clarity needed to align your life with your deepest motivations and embark on a purpose-driven path.

Defining Your Purpose Statement

Once you have identified the essence of your "why," the next step is to craft a purpose statement—a concise declaration that encapsulates your life's purpose. Your purpose statement serves as a guiding light, a mantra, and a reminder of the mission that propels you forward. It is a beacon of clarity that keeps you on course when life's storms threaten to obscure your vision.

In this section, we will delve into the art of crafting a purpose statement that is both meaningful and actionable. We will explore the key elements that make up a purposeful declaration and provide you with tools and exercises to help you refine and articulate your purpose. Your purpose statement will serve as a touchstone throughout your journey, reminding you of your unique path and helping you make decisions that align with your purpose.

As we venture deeper into the exploration of clarity, remember that this is just the beginning of your

purpose-driven odyssey. By the end of this chapter, you will have taken significant strides toward understanding your "why" and defining your purpose statement. These newfound insights will become the foundation upon which we build the framework for your purposeful life.

Prepare to embark on this illuminating journey, for the power of clarity will set you on a course toward a life filled with intention, fulfillment, and the profound sense of purpose you seek.

The Art of Crafting a Purpose Statement

A purpose statement is the compass that guides your life, providing direction, motivation, and clarity about your mission. It serves as a roadmap for your actions, decisions, and aspirations. Crafting a purpose statement that is both meaningful and actionable is an art that requires introspection, reflection, and precision. Here, we'll explore the key elements that make up a purposeful declaration and introduce tools and exercises to help you refine and articulate your purpose.

Key Elements of a Purpose Statement

Clear and Concise Language: Your purpose statement should be clear and concise, free from ambiguity. It should communicate your core mission in a straightforward manner that is easy to understand.

Reflects Your Values: Your purpose should be in alignment with your values and beliefs. It should reflect what truly matters to you and what you stand for.

Inspiring and Motivating: A purpose statement should inspire and motivate you to take action. It should be a source of energy and enthusiasm for pursuing your goals.

Actionable: Your purpose statement should contain actionable language, indicating what you will do or how you will contribute to the world. It should not be vague or passive.

Timeless: A purpose statement is not time-bound; it should remain relevant throughout your life. It represents a long-term mission that transcends specific goals or timeframes.

Tools and Exercises for Crafting Your Purpose Statement

Self-Reflection: Begin by reflecting on your life, experiences, and values. What activities or moments have brought you the greatest joy or fulfillment? Which problems or causes have a strong emotional resonance for you? This introspection forms the foundation of your purpose.

Journaling: Keep a journal to capture your thoughts and insights as you explore your purpose. Write about your passions, dreams, and the impact you want to make in the world. Journaling allows you to refine your ideas and gain clarity.

Values Assessment: Identify your core values. There are various values assessment tools available online that can help you pinpoint the values that are most

important to you. Understanding your values is essential for aligning them with your purpose.

Mind Mapping: Create a mind map to visually represent your purpose. Start with a central idea, such as "My Purpose," and branch out with associated words, phrases, and concepts. This can help you see the interconnectedness of your mission.

Visualization: Close your eyes and visualize your ideal future—a life lived in alignment with your purpose. What does it look like? How do you feel? Visualization can help you paint a vivid picture of your mission.

Writing Exercises: Experiment with writing exercises like "I am..." statements. Complete the sentence "I am here to..." multiple times with different endings to explore various aspects of your purpose.

Feedback and Discussion: Share your purpose exploration with trusted friends, mentors, or family members. Their feedback and insights can offer fresh perspectives and help you refine your purpose statement.

Multiple Drafts: Crafting a purpose statement often involves multiple drafts and revisions. Don't be

discouraged by the initial versions. Each iteration brings you closer to a purpose statement that truly resonates.

Remember that your purpose statement is a dynamic document that can evolve as you gain new insights and experiences. It's a declaration of your authentic self and the positive impact you wish to have on the world. Crafting it is an artful and deeply personal process, and the journey of self-discovery it entails is as valuable as the final statement itself. So, take your time, explore your innermost desires, and embrace the art of crafting a purpose statement that guides you toward a life of meaning and fulfillment.

Chapter 2

Law 1 - Aligning with Your Values

In the grand tapestry of our lives, our values are the threads that weave our moral fabric, shaping our beliefs, decisions, and actions. Law #1, "Aligning with Your Values," is the first pillar on our journey to purpose attainment. In this chapter, we will delve into the importance of discovering your core values and the transformative power of living in alignment with them.

Discovering Your Core Values

Your core values are the deeply ingrained beliefs that define who you are and what you stand for. They are the compass by which you navigate life's complex terrain, guiding you toward what resonates most with your true self. Yet, many of us may not have taken the time to introspect and identify these guiding principles consciously.

In this section, we will embark on a voyage of self-discovery. We will explore techniques and exercises to help you unearth your core values, those principles that lie at the heart of your being. Understanding these values is crucial, as they form the foundation upon which your purpose is built. By gaining clarity on your values, you will gain insight into what truly matters to you and set the stage for a life lived authentically.

Living in Alignment

Once you've identified your core values, the next step is to bring your life into harmony with them. Living in alignment with your values means making choices and taking actions that are congruent with your deepest beliefs. When you do this, you create a sense of inner harmony and fulfillment.

In this part of the chapter, we will explore practical strategies for aligning your daily life with your core values. We'll discuss how to make decisions that are in line with your values and how to create a life that reflects your true self. You'll discover that living in alignment not only brings a sense of purpose but also reduces inner conflict and fosters a greater sense of well-being.

As we dive into Law 1, you'll realize that aligning with your values is not just a philosophical concept; it is a powerful force that can transform your life. It will serve as the cornerstone upon which you build a purposeful existence. By the end of this chapter, you will have the tools and understanding to begin the process of discovering your core values and taking the steps necessary to live in alignment with them, setting the stage for a life of deeper meaning and fulfillment.

Practical Strategies for Aligning Your Daily Life with Your Core Values

Living in alignment with your core values involves making conscious choices and taking deliberate actions that reflect these values in your daily life. Here are practical strategies to help you ensure that your decisions and actions are in line with your values and that your life reflects your true self:

Identify Your Core Values: As discussed earlier, the first step is to clearly define your core values. Create a list of your most important values, such as honesty, integrity, family, community, personal growth, or adventure.

Prioritize Your Values: Not all values are of equal importance. Rank your values in order of priority. This will help you make decisions when values conflict, as you'll know which one takes precedence.

Set Clear Goals: Align your goals with your core values. Whether your goals are related to career, relationships, or personal development, ensure that they resonate with your values. For example, if family is a core value, set goals that prioritize spending quality time with loved ones.

Create a Vision Board: Visual representations of your goals and values can serve as powerful reminders. Create a vision board with images and words that symbolize your values and aspirations.Put it in a place where you can see it every day.

Practice Mindfulness: Regularly reflect on your values and how they relate to your daily life. Mindfulness meditation can help you stay in touch with your inner values and guide your decisions accordingly.

Set Boundaries: Establish boundaries that protect your values. If, for instance, work is interfering with your family time (a core value), set limits on your work hours to ensure you allocate quality time to your loved ones.

Engage in Values-Based Decision-Making: When faced with important decisions, consciously evaluate how each option aligns with your values."Does this choice honor my core values?" is a question you should ask yourself. This straightforward query can provide direction.

Seek Guidance from Your Values: Use your values as a compass in challenging situations. When you're uncertain about a decision, consult your values to help you make choices that resonate with your true self.

Surround Yourself with Like-Minded People: Build relationships with individuals who share your values or respect them. Associating with people who align with your values can provide support and reinforcement.

Reflect and Adjust: Periodically assess your life and determine if it reflects your values and authentic self. If you find areas where you've strayed from alignment, make adjustments to bring your life back into harmony with your values.

Practice Gratitude: Regularly express gratitude for the aspects of your life that align with your values. Gratitude can reinforce your commitment to living authentically.

Stay Open to Growth: Be open to evolving your values as you grow and gain new insights. Your values may evolve, and it's important to adapt your life accordingly.

Remember that aligning with your core values is an ongoing process, and it may require courage and self-reflection. However, the rewards of living a life that reflects your true self and aligns with your values are profound, leading to a sense of purpose, fulfillment, and inner peace.

Chapter 3

Law 2 - Setting Clear Goals

In our journey to purpose attainment, having a destination in mind is paramount. Law #2, "Setting Clear Goals," serves as a critical milestone on this path. In this chapter, we explore the art and science of goal setting, uncovering the transformative power of defining and pursuing clear objectives.

SMART Goal Setting

Setting goals is an art that, when done effectively, can transform dreams into realities. The acronym SMART serves as a valuable guide in crafting clear and actionable goals. Each letter represents a key characteristic of a well-defined goal:

S - Specific: Your goal should be specific and well-defined. Vague objectives make it challenging to measure progress and success. Instead of saying, "I want to be successful," specify what success means to you and how you will achieve it.

M - Measurable: Goals should be measurable to track your progress and know when you've achieved them. How will I know when I've accomplished my goal? is a question to ask oneself. Define concrete criteria for success.

A - Achievable: While it's essential to aim high, goals should also be realistic. Ensure that your objectives are attainable given your resources, time, and capabilities. Set challenging but doable targets.

R - Relevant: Your objectives ought to be in line with your values and desires. They should be relevant to your overall purpose. Ensure that pursuing the goal will bring you closer to your desired life.

T - Time-Bound: Set a specific timeframe for your goals. A deadline instills a sense of urgency and aids in task prioritization. Rather than stating, "I will learn a new language someday," for instance, say, "I will learn French within the next six months."

Breaking Down Big Goals

While ambitious, long-term goals are inspiring, they can also be overwhelming. To make them manageable and less intimidating, it's essential to break them down into smaller, actionable steps. This process is known as "chunking" or "goal decomposition."

In this section, we explore the practical aspects of breaking down big goals into smaller, more achievable tasks:

Start with the End in Mind: Begin by clearly defining your long-term goal. What is the outcome you desire? This provides clarity and motivation.

Identify Milestones: Break your long-term goal into smaller milestones or sub-goals. These are significant steps that mark your progress.

Set Deadlines: Assign deadlines to each milestone. Having specific timeframes ensures that you stay on track and maintain focus.

Create Action Plans: For each milestone, outline the specific actions required to achieve it. Think about the tools, abilities, and assistance you require.

Prioritize Tasks: Determine the sequence in which you will tackle each task. Prioritization ensures that you address the most critical aspects first.

Monitor Progress: Regularly review your progress. Celebrate accomplishments, revise and adjust your plans as needed. It's normal to adapt as you gain new insights.

Stay Flexible: Be willing to modify your objectives and goals as necessary as events unfold. Life is dynamic, and flexibility is a valuable trait in goal pursuit.

By breaking down big goals into manageable pieces and applying the SMART criteria, you empower yourself to make consistent progress while maintaining a clear sense of direction. In the journey of purpose attainment, setting clear goals is akin to plotting the course on a map—it guides your steps and keeps your vision alive. Through the application of these principles, you will discover that the pursuit of your purpose becomes not only attainable but also profoundly rewarding.

Chapter 4

Law 3 - Cultivating Self-Awareness

In our quest for purpose attainment, self-awareness serves as the compass that guides us through the intricate terrain of our inner world. Law #3, "Cultivating Self-Awareness," is the essential foundation upon which personal growth and self-realization are built. In this chapter, we embark on the journey within, exploring the profound significance of self-awareness and the transformative power it holds.

The Journey Within

The journey within is a profound expedition into the depths of your being—a pilgrimage to understand your thoughts, emotions, desires, and motivations. It is a process of peeling back the layers of self, uncovering your true essence, and gaining insights into the intricacies of your inner world.

In this section, we delve into the journey within and explore why self-awareness is crucial on the path to purpose attainment:

Reflective Practices: We'll discuss various techniques and exercises, such as meditation, journaling, and mindfulness, that can help you develop self-awareness. These practices allow you to observe your thoughts and emotions without judgment, providing valuable insights into your inner landscape.

Emotional Intelligence: Understanding and managing your emotions is a critical aspect of self-awareness. We'll explore how emotional intelligence can enhance your relationships, decision-making, and overall well-being.

Self-Discovery: The journey within is a process of self-discovery. You will learn to recognize your values, passions, and aspirations, gaining clarity on what truly matters to you. Self-discovery is an essential step in aligning your life with your purpose.

Embracing Your Strengths and Weaknesses

Self-awareness extends beyond understanding your thoughts and emotions—it also involves acknowledging your strengths and weaknesses. Embracing these aspects of yourself is essential for personal growth and purpose attainment.

In this part of the chapter, we explore how to embrace your strengths and weaknesses:

Strengths: We'll discuss the importance of recognizing and leveraging your strengths. Your strengths are the unique qualities and talents that empower you to excel in certain areas. Embracing and developing your strengths can lead to greater self-confidence and success.

Weaknesses: Acknowledging your weaknesses is a sign of self-awareness and humility. We'll explore how to work on your weaknesses and turn them into areas of growth. Understanding your limitations can lead to personal development and resilience.

Self-Acceptance: Ultimately, self-awareness is about self-acceptance. It's about embracing your whole self, with both strengths and weaknesses. When you accept yourself as you are, you pave the way for personal growth and a more profound sense of purpose.

As you embark on the journey of self-awareness, you will gain profound insights into your true self, uncover your unique strengths and weaknesses, and find the keys to unlocking your purpose. The path may be introspective and at times challenging, but the rewards are immeasurable—a deeper connection with yourself and a greater capacity to live a life aligned with your true calling. Through the exploration of Law #3, you will come to understand that cultivating self-awareness is not only a step on the path to purpose but a destination in itself—a journey worth embarking upon.

Chapter 5

Law 4 - Building Resilience

In the pursuit of purpose, resilience is the bedrock upon which we weather life's storms and emerge stronger and wiser. Law 4, "Building Resilience," stands as a critical pillar in our journey toward purpose attainment. In this chapter, we explore the transformative power of resilience, delving into the art of overcoming challenges and learning from setbacks.

Overcoming Challenges

Life, with all its beauty and wonder, is also a terrain fraught with challenges and obstacles. These challenges can take many forms, from personal hardships to external adversities. However, it is not the presence of challenges that defines our journey but how we respond to them.

In this section, we explore the strategies and mindset needed to overcome challenges:

Positive Mindset: Resilience begins with a positive and growth-oriented mindset. We will discuss how cultivating optimism and reframing challenges as opportunities for growth can empower you to navigate adversity.

Adaptability: The ability to adapt to changing circumstances is a key aspect of resilience. We'll explore how flexibility and problem-solving skills can help you respond effectively to unexpected challenges.

Seeking Support: Building a support network is crucial when facing challenges. We'll discuss the importance of seeking help from friends, family, or professionals when needed and how this strengthens resilience.

Learning from Setbacks

Setbacks are an inevitable part of any journey, including the journey to purpose attainment. However, setbacks need not be viewed as failures but rather as valuable learning experiences. They offer opportunities for growth, self-discovery, and resilience.

In this part of the chapter, we delve into the process of learning from setbacks:

Reflection: We'll explore the importance of reflection when setbacks occur. Taking the time to assess what went wrong, what you learned, and how you can improve sets the stage for future success.

Adapting and Rebounding: Resilience is not about avoiding failure but about bouncing back from it. We'll discuss strategies for adapting to setbacks and using them as stepping stones toward your purpose.

Embracing Perseverance: Perseverance is a core component of resilience. We'll explore how maintaining your determination and focus, even in the face of setbacks, can lead to long-term success.

Through the exploration of Law 4, you will come to understand that resilience is not the absence of adversity but the capacity to rise above it. It is a skill that can be cultivated and honed, enabling you to overcome challenges and learn from setbacks. As you navigate the terrain of resilience, you will find that each obstacle you encounter is not an impediment but an opportunity—a chance to strengthen your resolve and move closer to your purpose. By embracing this law, you are equipping yourself with the tools to face life's challenges with courage and grace, ultimately propelling you further on your path to purpose attainment.

Chapter 6

Law 5 - Nurturing Relationships

In the intricate tapestry of our lives, relationships are the threads that weave together our experiences, emotions, and sense of purpose. Law #5, "Nurturing Relationships," is a pivotal cornerstone on our journey to purpose attainment. In this chapter, we explore the profound significance of relationships, uncovering the transformative power of connection and the importance of surrounding yourself with support.

The Power of Connection

Human beings are inherently social creatures, and our lives are enriched by the connections we forge with others. These connections not only provide companionship but also offer opportunities for growth, learning, and shared purpose.

In this section, we delve into the power of connection and its impact on our pursuit of purpose:

Emotional Support: We'll discuss how nurturing relationships can provide emotional support during both the highs and lows of life. Genuine connections can bolster your resilience and overall well-being.

Shared Experiences: Relationships often involve shared experiences, and these shared moments can be instrumental in shaping your understanding of your purpose. We'll explore how the stories, challenges, and triumphs of others can influence your journey.

Collaboration and Inspiration: Connections can spark collaboration and inspiration. Engaging with like-minded individuals who share your values and passions can amplify your efforts and ignite your sense of purpose.

Surrounding Yourself with Support

While relationships can bring joy and support, it's also important to be intentional about the company you keep. Surrounding yourself with individuals who uplift and encourage you on your purposeful path is a key aspect of Law 5.

In this part of the chapter, we discuss how to create a supportive network:

Identifying Positive Influences: Recognize individuals who inspire and empower you. These may be friends, mentors, or colleagues who align with your values and aspirations.

Setting Boundaries: Establish healthy boundaries in your relationships. Protect your time and energy by prioritizing connections that align with your purpose and values.

Giving and Receiving: Healthy relationships involve a balance of giving and receiving support. Be willing to provide support to others as well, as it strengthens the bonds of connection.

Seeking Mentorship: Consider seeking mentorship from individuals who have achieved what you aspire to. Mentorship can provide valuable guidance and accelerate your progress.

Community Engagement: Engage with communities and organizations that resonate with your purpose. These groups can offer a sense of belonging and shared purpose.

Through the exploration of Law 5, you will come to understand that relationships are not merely external factors in your life but integral components of your purpose journey. They provide a mirror in which you can see your values and aspirations reflected, and they offer a network of support and inspiration. By nurturing relationships and surrounding yourself with those who uplift and empower you, you are cultivating an environment in which your purpose can thrive. As you delve into this law, you will discover that the power of connection is not only a source of strength but also a catalyst for realizing your true purpose in the world.

Chapter 7

Law 6 - Taking Purposeful Action

In the grand tapestry of purpose attainment, action is the loom upon which we weave our aspirations into reality. Law 6, "Taking Purposeful Action," is a pivotal chapter on our journey, emphasizing the transformative power of action and the importance of creating a solid action plan while maintaining unwavering consistency.

Creating an Action Plan

A clear action plan is a blueprint that turns your dreams into tangible steps. It provides structure, direction, and a roadmap for your purposeful journey. Without a plan, even the most passionate aspirations may remain dormant.

In this section, we explore the essential elements of creating an action plan:

Defining Clear Objectives: Clearly articulate the specific goals and milestones you aim to achieve on your purposeful path. Ensure that your objectives are in alignment with your purpose and values.

Breaking Down Tasks: Divide your goals into smaller, manageable tasks. This breakdown not only makes your goals more achievable but also helps you maintain focus and momentum.

Setting Deadlines: Assign realistic deadlines to each task and milestone. Deadlines provide a sense of urgency and accountability, motivating you to stay on track.

Resource Allocation: Identify the resources, skills, and support you need to accomplish your goals. Whether it's time, money, knowledge, or assistance from others, consider what is required.

Measuring Progress: Establish key performance indicators (KPIs) or metrics to track your progress. Regularly assess how you're advancing toward your goals and make adjustments as needed.

Staying Consistent

The thread of consistency is what moves the fabric of success. Taking purposeful action requires commitment and persistence. It's not just about starting; it's about maintaining the momentum and pushing through challenges.

In this part of the chapter, we delve into the strategies for staying consistent:

Establishing Habits: Transforming actions into habits can make consistency more manageable. Choose habits that will help you achieve your goals and incorporate them into your regular activities.

Accountability: Share your goals with a trusted friend, mentor, or coach who can hold you accountable. Regular check-ins and discussions about your progress can keep you motivated.

Embracing Perseverance: Understand that setbacks and obstacles are part of the journey. Maintain your determination and resilience, even when faced with challenges.

Celebrate Your Small Successes: Recognize and enjoy Your Successes Along the Way. Recognizing your progress, no matter how small, can boost motivation and morale.

Visualization: Visualize your success and the positive impact your actions will have on your life and the lives of others. Visualization can help you maintain a clear sense of purpose.

By embracing Law 6, you will recognize that purposeful action is the bridge between your aspirations and their realization. Creating a well-structured action plan and staying consistent in your efforts are the keys to transforming your purpose from a distant dream into a tangible reality. As you navigate this law, you will discover that taking purposeful action is not just a task; it is a way of life—a commitment to living in alignment with your deepest values and aspirations.

Chapter 8

Law 7 - Finding Fulfillment

In the grand culmination of our purposeful journey, Law 7, "Finding Fulfillment," stands as the ultimate destination—a place where the threads of our purpose weave together to form a tapestry of profound meaning and significance. In this chapter, we explore the transformative power of fulfillment and the significance of leaving a legacy.

The Ultimate Reward

Fulfillment is the crown jewel of purpose attainment, the sweet fruit of your labor, and the sense of contentment that arises from living in alignment with your true purpose. It is the feeling that you are on the right path, that your actions matter, and that your life has meaning.

In this section, we explore the elements that contribute to finding fulfillment:

Living with Purpose: Fulfillment arises from a life lived with intention and purpose. We'll discuss how aligning your actions with your values and aspirations can lead to a profound sense of fulfillment.

Inner Peace: When you are living in harmony with your purpose, inner peace becomes a natural byproduct. The absence of inner conflict and a sense of contentment are hallmarks of fulfillment.

Joy and Gratitude: Fulfillment often brings joy and gratitude for the opportunities and experiences that your purposeful life affords you. These positive emotions become part of your daily existence.

Leaving a Legacy

Beyond personal fulfillment, the impact of a purposeful life extends to the world around you. Leaving a legacy is about the lasting influence you create, the positive mark you leave on others, and the ripple effect of your actions.

In this part of the chapter, we delve into the significance of leaving a legacy:

Impact on Others: We'll explore how your purposeful actions can inspire and influence those around you. Your values and commitment can serve as a beacon for others seeking their paths.

Contributing to Society: Leaving a legacy often involves contributing to the greater good of society. We'll discuss how your actions can address societal needs and challenges, leaving a positive imprint.

Transcending Time: A legacy is not bound by time; it extends beyond your lifetime. We'll reflect on the enduring impact you can have on future generations, inspiring them to live purposefully.

By embracing Law 7, you will come to understand that fulfillment is the culmination of your purposeful journey, the reward for living in alignment with your values and aspirations. It is a state of being that radiates from within, touching not only your own life but the lives of those you encounter. Leaving a legacy is the final brushstroke on the canvas of your purpose—a testament to the impact you've made and the lasting change you've created. As you explore this law, you will discover that finding fulfillment and leaving a legacy are not just end goals; they are the enduring legacy of a life well-lived, a life of purpose and significance.

Conclusion

Embracing Your Purposeful Journey

As we reach the closing chapter of this transformative exploration, we stand at the threshold of profound discovery—the discovery of your purposeful self. Through the Seven Laws of Purpose Attainment, we have traversed a landscape of self-awareness, resilience, connection, and action, uncovering the wisdom and insights needed to guide you on your unique path.

Embracing your purposeful journey is not merely a destination but a lifelong commitment—a commitment to living a life of intention, authenticity, and meaning. It is a pledge to yourself, a recognition that your existence is not a mere accident but a deliberate opportunity to contribute to the world in a way that only you can.

Throughout this journey, you have delved deep into the core of your being, unraveling the threads of your values, passions, and aspirations. You have harnessed the power of resilience to overcome challenges and setbacks, understanding that they are not roadblocks but stepping stones. You have forged connections, creating a web of support and inspiration that strengthens your pursuit of purpose. And you have taken purposeful action, weaving your dreams into the fabric of reality, one deliberate step at a time.

Embracing your purposeful journey is an ongoing commitment—a commitment to revisit your values, adapt to change, and grow with each new experience. It is a promise to yourself that, no matter the obstacles or distractions that may arise, you will stay true to your course and continue to seek fulfillment.

Your journey has not been in vain; it has been a journey of self-discovery, transformation, and empowerment. As you stand here today, you are equipped with the tools, insights, and understanding needed to navigate the twists and turns of life with purpose and grace.

But remember, your purposeful journey is not meant to be traveled in isolation. Share your wisdom, support others on their paths, and leave a legacy that inspires future generations to embrace their unique purpose.

In closing, know that your journey is as unique as your fingerprint, and its unfolding is a gift to the world. Embrace it with open arms, let your purpose shine brightly, and live a life that leaves an indelible mark on the tapestry of existence. You are the author of your story, the weaver of your purpose, and the bearer of a light that can illuminate the world. So, go forth with courage, conviction, and a heart filled with purpose, and may your journey be a source of inspiration and fulfillment.